Susan's Special CHRISTMAS

By
Mason Ellis
A g e 1 0

HARVEST
HOUSE
PUBLISHERS

Eugene, Oregon 97402

Copyright © 1997
by Harvest House Publishers
Eugene, Oregon 97402

Library of Congress Cataloging–in–Publication Data

Ellis, Mason, 1983–
    Susan's special Christmas / Mason Ellis.
        p. cm.
    Summary: Greedy Susan has a special visit from Santa Claus
in which she learns the true meaning of Christmas.
    ISBN 1–56507–608–7
    [1. Christmas—Fiction. 2. Children's writings. 3. Stories in
rhyme.] I. Title.
PZ8.3.E4956Su   1997   96–53953
[E]—dc21   CIP
                                                AC

Design and production by
Left Coast Design, Portland, Oregon

Artwork that appears in this book is from
the personal collection of Alda Ellis.

Printed in the United States of America.

97 98 99 00 01 02 03 04 05 06 / BG / 10 9 8 7 6 5 4 3 2 1

The Most Wonderful Present

It seems like only yesterday.
It was Christmas Day 1993,
and that particular Christmas I
received the most wonderful present.

Christmas dinner that year was a traditional
gathering of grandparents, aunts, uncles, nieces, and
nephews. We all sat in the dining room, elbow to
elbow. The table had been extended, an extra children's
table added, and we even had a high chair.

We feasted together on
turkey with all the
trimmings, and
for dessert—
Grandmother's
raisin and
coconut pies.

As dinner drew to a close, I found myself enjoying one of those moments you look forward to all year. The shopping was done. The presents had been wrapped and opened. The holiday meal was over, and it was just the time to sit back and realize that what we had worked on for so long was over so quickly.

Before we all got up from the table, I felt a little tap on my shoulder. It was my ten-year-old son, Mason. "Here, Mama. Here's your Christmas present I made you."

He handed me a neat little square of notebook paper, folded several times and tied up with a red ribbon (from earlier that morning). "I wrote this for you," he said.

As I unfolded the paper, the family conversation hushed. Through the wrinkles in the paper I saw my son's handwriting, and I began to read aloud the story of Susan's Special Christmas. . .

Susan's Special
CHRISTMAS

It's Christmas Eve!
It's Christmas Eve!
Time to rejoice!

It's Christmas Eve!
It's Christmas Eve!
Time to make noise.
Church bells are ringing,
Everyone's singing.
Time to be happy!

Little girl Susan,
A greedy young girl—
Why, last Christmas
She wanted a big, ten-foot pearl!

It was eleven-thirty,
As Susan laid on the couch.

Except for the clock,
There wasn't a sound.

Susan was still awake,
When she heard a noise.
She saw a bag come down
the chimney,
A bag full of toys!

She hollered,
hooted, and howled.
"It's Santa! It's Santa!"
she said, very loud.
She jumped off
the couch,
And to the man in red,
"What did you bring me?
What did you bring me?" she said.

Santa spoke,
"Why aren't
you in bed?"

"Ha! And miss you bringing
all those toys to me?
I've been a good girl."
(Or has she?)
"Toys, toys, toys, toys!"
She said out loud.

"Come with me," said Old Saint Nick,
"I'm taking you back a long time ago,
So you can see the true
meaning of Christmas
And the star that shown
A long time ago in Bethlehem.

"There was a lady and a man,
And God told to an angel,
Who then told to Mary,
'You are going to have
a baby to carry.'

"Gabriel was the angel's name
Who told to Mary
About the tiny babe,
Who would be the Savior,
the new King.

The angels rejoiced and started to sing.
"But enough about talking," Santa said,
"Let's go see it.
O, by the way, you better put on your mitts!"

So Susan and Santa hopped in the sled.
"Now when I say duck,
You duck your head!
We're going back to Bible days," Santa said.

Santa said,
"What do you think
Christmas is about?"

Then she saw it—
The shepherds,
the wise men,
The bright,
beautiful star,
Joseph and
Mary and
Jesus the
King.
She saw
it all.

Santa said,
"Now you see
Christmas isn't
about presents.
It isn't about me.
It's about Jesus the King,
The King who saves us from sin,
Who was born long ago
In Bethlehem."

The next morning
Susan found out
She was in
the same place as before,
On the new, fluffy couch.
She got up, and she looked on the floor.
She saw presents and presents
Tucked under the tree, gifts and more gifts.
She looked out the window,
And the trip with Saint Nick
She started to miss,
Along with the star that flickered
and flicked, And the Savior
that was born
Long time ago
In Bethlehem.

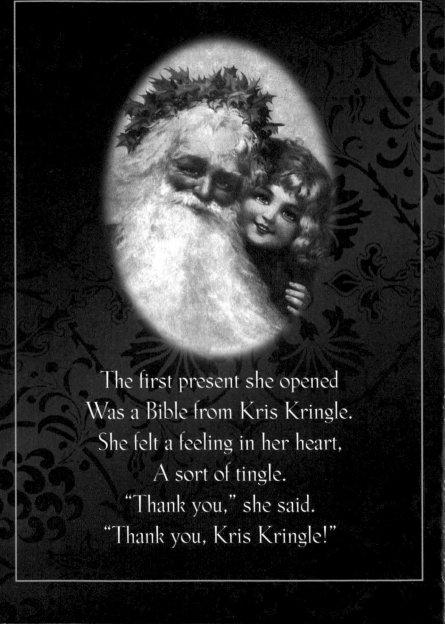

The first present she opened
Was a Bible from Kris Kringle.
She felt a feeling in her heart,
A sort of tingle.
"Thank you," she said.
"Thank you, Kris Kringle!"